Native American Library

# CREE
## History and Culture

Helen Dwyer and Mary Stout

Consultant Robert J. Conley
Sequoyah Distinguished Professor at Western Carolina University

**Gareth Stevens**
Publishing

**Please visit our website, www.garethstevens.com. For a free color catalog of all our high-quality books, call toll free 1-800-542-2595 or fax 1-877-542-2596.**

**Library of Congress Cataloging-in-Publication Data**

Dwyer, Helen.
Cree history and culture / Helen Dwyer and Mary Stout.
  p. cm. — (Native American library)
Includes index.
ISBN 978-1-4339-7418-2 (pbk.)
ISBN 978-1-4339-7419-9 (6-pack)
ISBN 978-1-4339-7417-5 (library binding)
1. Cree Indians—History—Juvenile literature. 2. Cree Indians—Social life and customs—Juvenile literature. I. Stout, Mary, 1954- II. Title.
E99.C88D95 2012
971.2004'97323—dc23

2011051634

New edition published in 2013 by
**Gareth Stevens Publishing**
111 East 14th Street, Suite 349
New York, NY 10003

First edition published 2005 by Gareth Stevens Publishing

Copyright © 2013 Gareth Stevens Publishing

Produced by Discovery Books
Project editor: Helen Dwyer
Designer and page production: Sabine Beaupré
Photo researchers: Tom Humphrey and Helen Dwyer
Maps: Stefan Chabluk

Photo credits: Corbis: pp. 15 (bottom), 18 (top), 21, 27 (top), 30, 32 (both), 34, 35, 36, 37, 38, 39; Getty Images: pp. 8 (William McFarlane Notman/George Eastman House), 31 (Mark Wilson); Courtesy of the Library of Congress: p. 11; North Wind Picture Archives: pp. 12, 14, 20; Peter Newark's American Pictures: pp. 13, 15 (top), 16 (both), 17, 18 (bottom), 19, 26 (top); Native Stock: pp. 22, 23 (both), 24 (bottom), 26 (bottom), 27 (bottom); Shutterstock: p. 5 (NatalieJean); Wikipedia: pp. 7 (Library of Congress), 28 (Masur), 29 (Cephas).

Printed in the United States of America

CPSIA compliance information: Batch #CS12GS: For further information contact Gareth Stevens, New York, New York at 1-800-542-2595.

# CONTENTS

Words that appear in the glossary are printed in **boldface** type the first time they appear in the text.

# INTRODUCTION

The Crees are a people of Alberta, Saskatchewan, Manitoba, Ontario, and Quebec in Canada and Montana in the United States. They are just one of the many groups of Native Americans who live today in North America. There are well over five hundred Native American tribes in the United States and more than six hundred in Canada. At least three million people in North America consider themselves to be Native Americans. But who are Native Americans, and how do the Crees fit into the history of North America's native peoples?

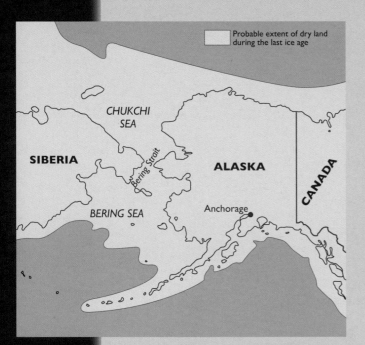

Siberia (Asia) and Alaska (North America) are today separated by an area of ocean named the Bering Strait. During the last ice age, the green area on this map was at times dry land. The Asian ancestors of the Crees walked from one continent to the other.

## THE FIRST IMMIGRANTS

Native Americans are people whose **ancestors** settled in North America thousands of years ago. These ancestors probably came from eastern parts of Asia. Their **migrations** probably occurred during cold periods called **ice ages**. At these times, sea levels were much lower than they are now. The area between northeastern Asia and Alaska was dry land, so it was possible to walk between the continents.

Scientists are not sure when these migrations took place, but it must have been more than twelve thousand years ago. Around that time, water levels rose and covered the land between Asia and the Americas.

The Cliff Palace at Mesa Verde, Colorado, is the most spectacular example of Native American culture that survives today. It consists of more than 150 rooms and pits built around A.D. 1200 from sandstone blocks.

By around ten thousand years ago, the climate had warmed and was similar to conditions today. The first peoples in North America moved around the continent in small groups, hunting wild animals and collecting a wide variety of plant foods. Gradually these groups spread out and lost contact with each other. They developed separate **cultures** and adopted lifestyles that suited their **environments.**

## SETTLING DOWN

Although many tribes continued to gather food and hunt or fish, some Native Americans began to live in settlements and grow crops. Their homes ranged from underground pit houses and huts of mud and thatch to dwellings in cliffs. By 3500 B.C., a plentiful supply of fish in the Pacific Ocean and in rivers had enabled people to settle in large coastal villages from Alaska to Washington State. In the deserts of Arizona more than two thousand years later, farmers constructed hundreds of miles of **irrigation** canals to carry water to their crops.

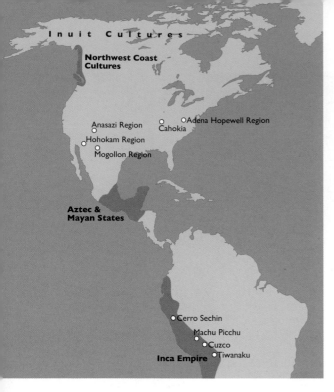

This map highlights some of the main early American cultures.

In the Ohio River valley between 700 B.C. and A.D. 500, people of the Adena and Hopewell cultures built clusters of large burial mounds, such as the Serpent Mound in Ohio, which survives today. In the Mississippi **floodplains**, the native peoples formed complex societies. They created mud and thatch temples on top of flat earth pyramids. Their largest town, Cahokia, in Illinois, contained more than one hundred mounds and may have been home to thirty thousand people.

The Crees followed a hunting and trapping lifestyle in the northern forests. Numerous lakes provided them with good opportunities for fishing as well. The Crees moved between winter hunting grounds and summer camps on lakeshores. In the warmer months, they gathered plant food to extend their diet.

## CONTACT WITH EUROPEANS

Around A.D. 1500, European ships reached North America. The first explorers were the Spanish. Armed with guns and riding horses, they took over land and forced the Native Americans to work for them. The Spanish were followed by the British, Dutch, and French, who were looking for land to settle and for opportunities to trade.

When Native Americans met these Europeans, they came into contact with diseases, such as **smallpox** and measles, that they had never experienced before. At least one half of all Native Americans, and possibly many more than that, were unable to overcome these diseases and died.

Guns were also disastrous for Native Americans. At first, only the Europeans had guns, which enabled them to overcome native peoples in fights and battles. Eventually, Native American groups obtained guns and used them in conflicts with each other. Native American groups were also forced to take sides and fight in wars between the French and British.

Horses, too, had a big influence in Native American lifestyles, especially on the Great Plains. Some groups became horse breeders and traders. People were able to travel greater distances and began to hunt buffalo on horseback. Soon horses became central to Plains trade and social life.

The Crees traded furs with the Hudson's Bay Company from 1670. In return, they received guns and horses. This allowed some Crees to change their lifestyle. They moved southwest onto the Great Plains and became buffalo hunters.

At the end of the 1700s, people of European descent began to migrate over the Appalachian Mountains, looking for new land to farm and exploit. By the middle of the nineteenth century, they had reached the West Coast of North America. This expansion was disastrous for Native Americans.

This portrait of a Cree woman was painted by Karl Bodmer, who traveled around America in the early 1830s.

## RESERVATION LIFE

Many native peoples were pressured into moving onto **reservations** to the west. The biggest of these reservations later became the U.S. state of Oklahoma. Native Americans who tried to remain in their homelands were attacked and defeated.

From 1850, American settlers killed off the great buffalo herds. The Plains Crees fought with other tribes over the few buffalo that were left. In the 1870s, they were forced to give up their lands. At the same time, lumber companies were moving into the far north, depriving the Western Woods (Woodland) Crees of their land. By 1906, all the Crees had been forced to give up their lands and move onto **reserves** in Canada. In the 1880s, one band of Plains Crees moved to Montana and joined together with an Ojibwe band. They became the Chippewa Crees, and their reservation was established in 1916.

New laws in the United States and Canada took away most of the control Native Americans had over their lives. They were expected to give up their cultures and adopt the ways and habits of white Americans. It became a crime to practice their traditional religions. Children were taken from their homes and placed in **boarding schools**, where they were forbidden to speak their native languages.

Despite this **persecution**, many Native Americans clung to their cultures through the first half of the twentieth century. The Society of American Indians was founded in 1911, and its campaign for U.S. citizenship for Native Americans was successful in 1924. Other Native American organizations were formed to promote traditional cultures and to campaign politically for Native American rights.

This photo of a Cree **travois** was taken in the 1880s.

# The Road to Self-Government

Despite these campaigns, Native Americans on reservations endured poverty and very low standards of living. Many of them moved away to work and live in cities, where they hoped life would be better. In most cases, they found life just as difficult. They not only faced **discrimination** and **prejudice** but also could not compete successfully for jobs against more established ethnic groups.

In the 1970s, the American Indian Movement (AIM) organized large protests that attracted attention worldwide. They highlighted the problems of unemployment, discrimination, and poverty that Native Americans experienced in North America.

The AIM protests led to changes in policy. Some new laws protected the civil rights of Native Americans, while other laws allowed tribal governments to be formed. Today tribal governments have a wide range of powers. They operate large businesses and run their own schools and health care.

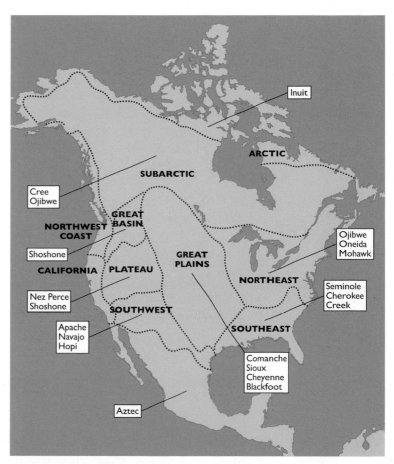

This map of North America highlights the main Native American cultural groups, along with the smaller groups, or tribes, featured in this series of books.

## Chapter 1

# LAND AND ORIGINS

## LAND OF THE CREES

The Cree **Nation** is made up of numerous small hunter-gatherer bands who once roamed a huge area in Canada east of the Hudson and James Bays, as far west as Alberta and as far south as Lake Superior. Today it is the largest Native American nation in Canada (where Indian tribes are called First Nations). Over 200,000 Crees live in Canada alone, and many others live in the United States.

As the orange areas show, before 1500, Cree territory stretched from what is today western Alberta to eastern Quebec in Canada. Some Cree bands gradually moved onto the Great Plains in what is now the northern United States.

## A TRADITIONAL ORIGIN STORY

Like many ancient peoples, for generations traditional Crees have told a story about how they came to their lands. In the beginning, the Crees lived in the land above. A man and a woman decided to go to the land below. As a spider lowered them on a line, it warned them not to look down until they reached the ground. Of course, they looked, so the line stopped, leaving them stuck atop a tall tree.

They asked a passing caribou, lynx, bear, and wolverine all to carry them down, but only the bear and wolverine would help. The couple followed the bear, which taught them everything about how to stay alive. According to this origin story, all the Crees are descended from these two.

The Ojibwe and French fur traders called them *Kristineaux,* later shortened to "Cree." The Crees called themselves "Nehiyawak," meaning "exact people."

The Cree tribe was divided into two major cultures. The culture of the Western Woods Crees, also called the Woodland Crees, was based upon hunting and trapping in the forests of the cold north. Buffalo hunting formed the basis of the Plains Crees' culture.

This Woodland Cree man is using a horn made of birch bark to imitate a moose call.

# The Cree Language

Cree is a Central Algonquian language with many different **dialects**.

| Cree | Pronunciation | English |
|------|---------------|---------|
| atim | uh-tim | dog |
| ta'n(i)si | tah-nih-sih | hello |
| tahka'ya'w | tuhk-ah-yow | (it's) cold |
| mispon | mis-pohn | snow |
| wa'skahikan | wah-skuh-hi-kun | house |

## Chapter 2

# HISTORY

## Western Woods Cree History

The Western Woods Crees included many different Cree bands. For hundreds of years, they lived off the land by hunting and trapping animals. Those living around the bays and lakes depended more upon fishing for food. All these bands spoke a similar language.

The huge demand for furs in Europe brought the first French traders to Cree country, where they set up trading posts. Excellent hunters and trappers, the Crees exchanged beaver pelts for trade goods, such as guns, knives, pots, pans, and other household items, first with the French and then with the British.

Trading posts also hired many Crees as hunters to supply them with meat. For a short time, the Crees were a rich, powerful tribe. As the supply of animals dwindled, however, the Crees had to keep moving south and west looking for more game. They were so busy hunting and trapping for the traders that many were no longer completely **self-sufficient** and became unable to live entirely off the land. By 1717,

During the 1800s, fur dealers arrived by wagon and boat at the Hudson's Bay trading post to buy and sell furs bound for Europe.

many Western Woods Crees depended upon the Hudson's Bay Company for guns, cloth, blankets, and for some of their food, changing their traditional lifestyle.

When Europeans arrived in North America, they brought diseases that killed more Native Americans than all other causes combined, including war. In 1781, a smallpox **epidemic** wiped out about half of the Cree population.

# Hudson's Bay Company

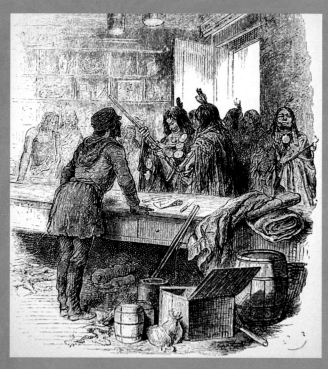

In this picture from 1845, Crees trade their furs for guns at the Hudson's Bay Company trading post.

In 1670, the British started the Hudson's Bay Company (HBC) in northern Canada to trade in furs for coats, hats, muffs, and capes. In 1821, HBC merged with its rival, the North West Company, and became the world's largest fur-trading business, expanding its territory throughout Canada. HBC governed a huge area and the natives living there until 1870, when it turned over all its lands to Canada.

HBC changed the lives of the Canadian natives, hiring them to trap and hunt and exchanging many European goods for furs and skins. Once beaver hats lost popularity in Europe in the mid-nineteenth century, the demand for furs declined. HBC became a successful Canadian department store, but native fur trappers lost both their jobs and the means to pay for the European goods they depended upon.

Jesuit missionaries coming to preach to the fur traders and Native Americans. Many had little respect for the traditional native spiritual practices they were trying to replace.

## CHANGES FOR THE WESTERN WOODS CREES

Native communities sprang up around trading posts, with religious **missions** located nearby; these areas became social centers and semipermanent homes for the formerly wandering Crees. The missionaries tried to **convert** the Western Woods Crees to Christianity. Giving up their traditional religion and lifestyle, many Crees also abandoned their traditional handmade goods for Canadian cloth, pots, pans, and other items.

Throughout the nineteenth century, however, few Europeans settled in the cold north, and the Indians continued to use their traditional hunting grounds. Then lumber companies disturbed the heavily forested lands. In **treaties** signed between 1876 and 1906, the Western Woods Crees traded most of their traditional lands to the Canadian government in exchange for reserves and promised **social services**.

From 1920 to 1940, many diseases new to the Crees, such as measles and flu, hit them hard. After World War II (1939–1945), government services such as schools and health clinics grew

> The Crees are more sprightly, always in motion, always dancing or singing. Both [Crees and Assiniboines] are brave and love war.
>
> *From a letter written in 1706 by Father Pierre-Gabriel Marest comparing the Assiniboine and Cree people*

Northern Crees traditionally came to the Great Whale River during the summer to hunt beluga whales, trade, and visit. These people were photographed in 1970.

up around the old trading posts, forming villages. The Crees lived in these villages year-round, though the men left on hunting trips during the winter.

By the 1940s, the Crees depended upon the Canadian government for their living. The market for fur was gone, and fewer Western Woods Crees lived in traditional ways. Beginning in the late 1940s until the 1970s, most Cree children were sent away to boarding schools where they learned English. Since they didn't live with their families, however, they forgot how to speak Cree and learned no traditional skills.

## Women's Work: Making Buckskin

The Western Woods Cree men depended upon Cree women to turn animal **hides** into leather for clothing. Women rubbed the animal hide with a mixture of animal brains, fat, and liver, and then soaked it in water. They softened the stiff hide by rubbing it over a rough stone, then stretched and pulled it. When the hide was soft, they could sew it into clothing — shirts, pants, and dresses. Once the Crees became dependent on woven cotton cloth, such traditional skills began to disappear.

A woman cleans a caribou hide at a Cree bush camp.

An 1826 painting by Peter Rindisbacher shows a Plains Cree man on foot chasing a buffalo with his dogs. Crees often hunted buffalo by frightening the animals so that they ran into pens or into a marsh, trapping them and making them easy targets.

## PLAINS CREE HISTORY

As the Crees expanded to their territory's southwest between 1670 and 1810, the Plains Crees emerged as a distinct group. The scarcity of winter game had forced them to move onto the Plains in southern Saskatchewan and Alberta to hunt buffalo.

They also became agents for the European traders, exchanging goods with other tribes for furs to bring into the trading posts.

**Allied** with the Blackfoot Indians, the Crees began to live like other Plains natives. Buffalo skins

Plains Cree families lived in tepees fashioned from twelve to twenty buffalo hides sewn together with **sinew** and supported by poles.

Mustatem Moutiapec (Horse Roots) was a Plains Cree Indian photographed at the turn of the twentieth century, after the buffalo had almost disappeared.

provided clothing and shelter, while buffalo meat fed the people. In the northern woods, the canoe had been the most important form of transportation, but for hunting on the Plains, horses were necessary.

Between 1810 and 1850, the Plains Crees moved farther into the Plains areas but had problems getting enough horses — both for transportation and, in their new lifestyle, for status. This time, known as the "Horse Wars," saw the Crees stealing or fighting to capture horses from other tribes.

## WARS AND TREATIES

Between 1850 and 1880, buffalo began to vanish from the Plains, killed by Americans for their hides. Because the animals disappeared first from Canada, the Crees entered other tribes' territories in the United States to hunt buffalo, which led to warfare. The Blackfeet drove the Crees out of their territory in today's southern Canada and northern Montana, defeating their former allies at the Battle of Old Man River in 1871.

Returning to Canada without buffalo, the starving Plains Crees requested a treaty with the Canadian government. In exchange for Cree lands, the treaty promised them farming tools, seeds, a yearly payment, and schools. Unfortunately, the government provided poor-quality grain and tools, so farming was difficult.

It may truly be said that they exist on the buffalo, and their knowledge of the habits of this animal is consequently essential to their preservation. . . . Next to the buffalo the horse is the mainstay of the prairie Indians. . . . Next to the horse, the dog is the Prairie Indians' most valuable friend.

*Professor Henry Youle Hind during his 1858 exploration, published in* Narrative of the Canadian Red River

## ALLYING WITH THE MÉTIS

In 1885, Louis Riel led the Métis (who were the **descendants** of Native Americans and Europeans, usually French) in an uprising against the Canadian government because it refused to admit that the Métis had any claims to the lands they had lived on all their lives. Plains Cree chiefs Poundmaker and Big Bear sympathized with the Métis. Some members of Big Bear's band killed nine priests and settlers at Frog Lake on the Alberta–Saskatchewan border. Eight Cree warriors were convicted of murder. Both Big Bear and Poundmaker were convicted of **treason** for planning to overthrow the Canadian government and sentenced to three years in prison. Big Bear's son led the rest of his band across the border to Montana, where they joined an Ojibwe (also known as Chippewa or Anishinaabe) band; their descendants continue to live there today.

Louis Riel spent his life fighting for the rights of the Métis.

This painting by Paul Kane shows Blackfoot chief Big Snake being killed by an unnamed Cree war chief. The Canadian artist created this work from his imagination; Big Snake actually died after the painting was completed.

By the late 1800s, Christian missionaries had become an important influence on the Plains Crees; they converted many to Christianity and worked to end traditional religious practices. From 1884 to 1921, for example, the Sun Dance was outlawed in Canada, and many other traditional ceremonies had to be held in secret. World War II (1939–1945) saw more and better social services for the Plains Crees, and returning war veterans became new leaders within the Cree community. Plains Cree children went to missionary schools, while their parents, no longer able to live off the land, looked to paying jobs and government allowances to help them survive.

## Poundmaker

Called Pitikwahanapiwiyin by the Crees, Poundmaker was adopted by a Blackfoot chief.

Poundmaker was born in 1842 and was named for his ability to make pens to trap buffalo, called "pounds." In 1876, he signed Treaty Number 6 with the Canadian government, but his band never received the food and farm tools promised in the treaty. The band then gave power to Fine Day, their war chief, who wished to join the Métis' fight against the government. Poundmaker opposed this, but the Canadian government accused him of treason anyway. He turned himself in and was found guilty at his two-day trial in 1885. Although he was sent to prison for three years, he was released early because of illness and died soon after in 1886.

# TRADITIONAL WAY OF LIFE

## Chapter 3

## WESTERN WOODS CREE TRADITIONAL CULTURE

When a Western Woods Cree child came into the world, there was little ceremony. Named several months after birth by an older person, the baby was often kept on a cradleboard with moss diapers. Young children were allowed to do as they liked, but as they grew older, they had to help their parents.

Western Woods Cree teenagers fasted alone for a short time to gain powers from the spirits that appeared in their dreams or **visions**. When a boy killed his first big-game animal, such as an elk or moose, at about age fourteen, a feast was held in his honor. A girl reaching **puberty** stayed in a small lodge away from camp for four nights with a wise old woman to keep her company and tell her stories. She returned to camp to attend a feast in her family lodge.

At first, Cree babies were carried in a hide sack stuffed with moss. The introduction of the cradleboard gave the Crees another way to carry their babies.

This early illustration of the Cree people shows life inside a traditional dwelling. The people warm themselves by the fire, which also cooks the meal in a pot and dries the meat hanging on a pole above.

## MOVING WITH THE SEASONS

The land of the Western Woods Crees is cold much of the year, so they traveled on snowshoes and toboggans during the long winter, as well as by canoes and dog travois in the summer. When everything froze, activity slowed, except when the men went hunting and trapping occasionally. Then, in spring, the Crees sprang into action for great caribou hunts. As soon as the rivers thawed, Cree bands paddled canoes to their summer camp, gathering at a lakeshore for fishing, berry picking, and visiting. By autumn, the bands would leave by canoe and scatter to their winter hunting grounds.

## DAILY LIFE

While the women set up camp, prepared meals, and took care of the young children, the men hunted and trapped caribou, moose, beaver, duck, and other game animals. Cree lodges — made of caribou hides covering a framework of wooden poles — provided shelter. Often decorated with porcupine quills or beads, most Cree clothing was made from the tanned hides of moose, caribou, and elk. Men wore moccasins, leggings, overshirts down to their knees, hats, mittens, and cloaks or blankets of beaver, caribou, or otter skins. Women dressed in moose-hide dresses and all the same warm outerwear as worn by the men.

# Body Decoration

Western Woods Crees used both tattooing and body paint as decoration. The men usually tattooed their chest and arms; women tattooed lines from their lower lip to their chin. Usually lines or shapes, the tattoos were made by putting a charcoal paste on the skin and then pricking it with needles. People painted their face with designs or with realistic figures, often using the color red.

A fire-making utensil case displays the beautiful decorative beadwork done by women on household items and clothing. Decorative work and tattooing often filled the time spent inside the lodges.

When the Western Woods Cree bands gathered together in the summertime, they worked hard but had a lot of fun. They played many games; both foot and horse races were popular. In the evenings, they told stories and sometimes held feasts and dances. Often the Crees painted and tattooed their faces and bodies with beautiful designs.

## GOVERNMENT AND RELIGION

The Western Woods Crees were organized into bands made up of family members; they had no formal government. Leaders were men chosen for their hunting ability, experience, and **spiritual** power. They tried to influence people's behavior but did not control it.

The Crees have kept many of their traditional religious beliefs private. They believed in a Great Spirit and feared the Windigo, a creature with a heart of ice and a taste for human flesh. The Crees believed that sickness and injuries were the results of evil spirits at work. Helping spirits, or manitous, came to them in dreams or visions and gave them special powers or protection for hunting or warfare.

Animals had spirits, too. The Crees believed that during the hunt, the hunter made a connection with the animal being hunted, and the animal decided whether or not to give itself to the hunter.

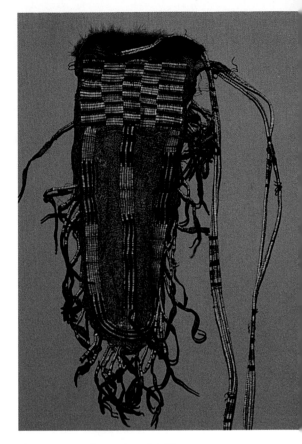

A copper hunting knife (left) and its beaded case are typical of the tools used by the early Crees.

## The Winter Windigo

A horrible creature, the gigantic Windigo comes at wintertime. Once a normal human being, the Windigo was taken over by a savage spirit and now wants to eat other humans. Though hairy on the outside, his body has ice on the inside. Only a **medicine man** or someone with special powers can kill a Windigo; that person must make sure to burn the Windigo as well so its heart of fire can be destroyed by fire.

## PLAINS CREE TRADITIONAL LIFE

A modern Cree medicine man, Oo-chin-a-pees. Keepers of traditional ways, Cree medicine men help heal people and provide spiritual leadership.

Soon after the birth of a Plains Cree baby, a medicine man or woman would name him or her, based on a vision or dream, at a feast. Parents might use a different "everyday" name with their child to protect its sacred given name.

Older children spent most of their time with their grandparents, who told them stories and taught them basic life skills. Teenage boys taught the younger ones how to hunt and fight. When girls went through puberty, they remained alone for four nights for their vision quest. Teenage boys also went on vision quests to seek spirit power, spending several nights alone while fasting. During a dream or vision, an animal spirit helper would appear, describe the gifts being given to the young man (such as the ability to lead war parties, cure the sick, or hunt buffalo), and teach him a power song.

The most important Plains Cree ceremony was the Sun Dance, given to honor the thunder or the sun. Also called the "Thirsting Dance" by the Crees, the participants did not eat or drink during the four-day ceremony but sang and danced throughout, concentrating

A braid of dried **sweetgrass** is burned, and the smoke purifies the people who breathe it.

24

A key religious ceremony, the Sun Dance was also a social event for the Cree people that featured dancing, gambling, and courting.

on keeping sacred promises, or vows, that were made to the spirits. During the Smoking Spirit ceremony, another important event, an all-night singing session honored all the spirits. Buffalo dances were held to assure large herds and good hunting. The Crees smoked a pipe as an offering to the **supernatural** and used sweat baths and the smoke from burning sweetgrass to clean and purify themselves.

## Shaking Tent

"Shaking tent" or "shaking lodge" is a practice in which a special medicine man enters a tent or lodge alone in order to speak with the spirits and find out the answers to questions that the people sitting outside might have. For example, if the hunters want to know where the buffalo are, the spirits are consulted. When the spirits enter the tent to speak with the medicine man, they cause the tent or lodge to move or sway from side to side.

A Cree chief, Broken Arm (also known as He-Who-Has-Eyes-Behind-Him) visited Washington, D.C., in 1831, where George Catlin painted his picture.

## PLAINS CREE GOVERNMENT

The Plains Crees were organized in groups of small bands, some of which had more than one chief. Councils of leading men made decisions for the band. Basing their decision on the chief's hunting ability, wealth, and generosity, people chose the band they wanted to join. Each band had a warrior society, to which most of the younger men belonged. The warrior society gave food to needy people and organized the large buffalo hunts.

## DEPENDING ON THE BUFFALO

Buffalo hides provided both clothing and shelter for the Plains Crees. Men wore hide **breechcloths** and leggings; women's dresses were also made of hide and decorated with beads

During the winter, the Crees wore mittens and moccasins made from hide and decorated with beadwork.

This shirt, decorated with battle scenes, was worn by a Plains Cree man on special ceremonial occasions.

or embroidery. Hide tepees provided housing.

Most of the food was based on the buffalo; when there was no fresh meat, the Crees ate **pemmican**. A typical Plains Cree meal was soup made from meat, fat, berries, and turnips. When the hunting was poor, the men fished and the women picked berries and dug wild turnips. Collecting maple sap, they made it into syrup and sugar.

## Cree Games: Early "Hoops"

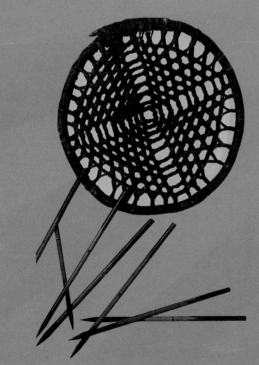

The Crees loved to play games and to gamble on their outcome. The men's hoop game was played with two teams who rolled between them a hoop with basketry strung inside of it. Meanwhile, the players shot arrows at it, trying to pin the hoop to the ground.

One popular gambling game used two small bones, one marked. One person would move the bones from hand to hand, while another tried to guess which closed hand held the marked bone.

# WESAKECHAK THE TRICKSTER

Many Cree stories are about the adventures of Wesakechak, a trickster hero similar to those in the legends of other Algonquian-speaking tribes. Wesakechak can change shape and become anything he wishes. He has the ability to speak to all plants and animals. He is also very greedy and is often looking for food.

Many of the stories told about Wesakechak are designed to explain the looks or behavior of different animals. For example, one story tells how a mouse helped Wesakechak. As a reward, the hero gave the mouse a pointed nose so that it could smell out its food better.

In other stories, animals play tricks on Wesakechak, so he punishes them. For example, the weasel suddenly stops running then listens and trembles because he thinks that Wesakechak is chasing him. In another story, the fox stole Wesakechak's meal and was punished by being surrounded by a ring of fire. The fox's fur was singed a bright red as he jumped over the fire.

On one occasion, Wesakechak captured some ducks to eat, but the ducks began to run away. Wesakechak kicked one of them and knocked its legs out of joint. This duck became the first grebe, and since that time, all grebes, like this western grebe, have had legs very far back on their body.

## GOOD AND BAD MANNERS

Most Cree stories emphasize the difference between good and bad behavior. The following story is all about greed and manners.

*A group of Crees lived near a lake, which contained an island with a colony of gulls. The gulls were always screaming at the people and swooping on them to scare them away. Around the village were trees that were home to a family of jays. They were quiet and friendly birds.*

*When the people pulled in their fishing nets and cleaned the fish, these two species of bird behaved very differently. The jays chatted quietly with the people and praised their fishing. The people liked the company of the birds and often gave them bits of food.*

The gray jay of this story lives in northern forests. The Crees know that this bird will come to camps looking for food and will even take food from a person's hand.

*The seagulls, however, were a nuisance. They flew down, screaming that the fish were theirs. If the people gave the gulls food, the birds fought over it. The people didn't want these noisy, aggressive neighbors, so they stopped giving the gulls food. Instead of being given all their food, the badly behaved gulls were forced to fly over the water looking for small scraps of fish.*

# CREES TODAY

## Chapter 4

## WORKING TOGETHER

During the last half of the twentieth century, European Canadians spread into traditional Cree hunting grounds and homelands, disturbing the Crees' traditional way of life. Instead of roaming the forests, Crees settled permanently onto numerous scattered reserves (reservations) in Canada and even one in the United States, as well as in many different Canadian cities and towns. They began to rely upon the Canadian government to provide education, housing, food, and medical care.

Realizing that the Canadian government had not followed through on its treaty promises, Crees became politically active in the 1960s. Plains Cree John Tootoosis founded and led the Federation of Saskatchewan Indians in 1958 and was active in the National Indian Brotherhood. These and other **activist** groups have worked hard to ensure that the Canadian government fulfilled all the rights listed in the treaties signed in exchange for Cree land.

Members of the National Indian Brotherhood and the Association of Indians meet together to discuss Cree land issues on November 19, 1974.

## GRAND COUNCIL OF THE CREES

The Crees of northern Quebec are represented by the Grand Council of the Crees. This council was set up in 1974. Today it works to promote the interests of the local Crees, such as preserving traditional lifestyles and improving conditions in Cree communities.

## CREES IN THE UNITED STATES

A group of Plains Crees fled to Montana in the 1880s and joined with an Ojibwe (Chippewa) band. In 1916, they were given the Rocky Boy Indian Reservation in northern Montana, only 40 miles (64 kilometres) from the Canadian border. In 1935, they were recognized by the U.S. government as the Chippewa Cree Tribe.

Today the tribe has more than five thousand members. In 2010, the population of the reservation was 3,323. The largest of the Chippewa Cree communities is Box Elder, with around 750 people. It is also one of the poorest, with more than half of the population living below the poverty line. In 2007, the tribe opened a casino, which provides around seventy jobs and is a considerable source of income for the tribe. The Chippewa Cree Tribe still celebrates traditional culture at gatherings several times each year, including an annual **powwow** in August.

U.S. President Barack Obama and Chippewa Cree Tribe Vice Chairman Jonathan Windy Boy shake hands after signing a new Tribal Law and Order Act at the White House in 2010.

## A Culture's Rebirth

A Canadian road sign tells drivers to stop in English, Cree symbols, and French.

Modern Cree children benefit from band and government programs to encourage Cree culture. Special Head Start Programs teach youngsters traditional singing, drumming, storytelling, and language in preschool. Many elementary schools teach kindergarten through third grades only in Cree, and some children now speak the language better than their parents. Other schools have hired Cree elders to advise them and hold powwows, feasts, and round dances during the school year. Cree groups sponsor older children in Cree culture camps during the summer, where they learn the skills needed to live off the land, or "bush skills," just as their great-grandparents had practiced.

In a bush camp near the Great Whale River, Cree women cook in the lodge just as their great-great-grandmothers did.

32

## CONTEMPORARY ARTS

Cree people participate in all the modern arts as well as continuing to work in traditional styles. Along with paintings and sculptures, Cree artists create moccasins, complex beadwork, and birch-bark boxes.

> How can we be discovered when we were already here?
>
> *Jane Ash Poitras, Cree artist*

Albertan author and artist George Littlechild illustrates children's picture books that he and others have written. One example is *This Land Is My Land*, a book that describes his experience of growing up as a Cree boy in Canada in colorful images and words.

Kent Monkman is a Cree painter and filmmaker from Manitoba who liked to paint and draw as a young boy. Now he uses Cree symbols — invented by a missionary in the late 1800s to express the Cree language — in a series of paintings called *The Prayer Language*. His first film, *A Nation Is Coming*, won several awards. He is working on more paintings and films that express a native point of view.

Jane Ash Poitras is a famous Cree artist from Alberta whose paintings hang in U.S. and Canadian museums. One of her works is a large exhibit that took three years to create. Called *Who Discovered the Americas?*, this mixture of preexisting images and paintings shows the effects of Columbus's "discovery" on Native Americans. Poitras's recent work also features the themes of native medicine and healing plants.

Allen Sapp was born on a reserve in Saskatchewan in 1928. His paintings portray scenes of Cree life from his early years. Sapp was honored as an Officer of the Order of Canada in 1986. His illustrations for the children's book *The Song Within My Heart* (2003) won the Governor General's Award.

# Buffy Sainte-Marie

Born February 20, 1941, on a Cree reserve in Saskatchewan, Canada, Buffy Sainte-Marie became a world-famous folksinger. While attending college, she became a popular singer on campus and in clubs. Sainte-Marie built a huge international following in the mid-1960s and became famous for an antiwar song called "Universal Soldier." During her career, she wrote over two hundred songs and recorded more than fifteen albums. In 1976, she left the music business to work as a teacher and an artist. She still does both and lives in Hawaii. She released two further albums, *Coincidence and Likely Stories* in 1992 and *Running for the Drum* in 2008.

Buffy Sainte-Marie has lived on many Native American/First Nation reservations during her life.

## REBUILDING A COMMUNITY

The Oujé-Bougoumou Crees live in northern Quebec. In the 1940s, outsiders arrived and set up mining operations on their land, a process that has gone on and increased ever since. The tribe has seen its villages destroyed and was relocated seven times up to 1970. Many of the habitats the tribe depended upon for food were also destroyed.

After many years of fighting for their rights, the Crees received money from the Quebec government to build a new, permanent village on the shores of Lake Opemisca. They chose the famous native architect Douglas Cardinal to design the village. The new buildings were influenced by traditional Cree structures. The houses have open beams, skylights, and doors that face east. The village's heating system uses waste sawdust from a local sawmill as a fuel in a central boiler house. This provides the whole village, both houses and public buildings, with heat and hot water through underground pipes.

The Aanischaaukamikw Cultural Institute was built in Oujé-Bougoumou in 2011. Its visible beams and curved shape mimic the traditional Cree gathering space where feasts were held.

Cree couple Anna and David Bosum set up a business offering cultural tours based around Oujé-Bougoumou. Visitors experience traditional Cree life while taking part in summer canoe trips.

# CREE ISSUES

## Chapter 5

## CONTEMPORARY CREE ISSUES

During the 1990s, the Canadian First Nations (including the Crees) and the Canadian government worked together to review the original treaties signed and settle any remaining treaty issues. This has resulted in many Cree bands signing a "Treaty Land Entitlement Agreement" and gaining additional lands in order to fulfill the original treaty agreement. Not all Cree bands have completed this process yet; it will probably take years.

More than one hundred years after Poundmaker was convicted of treason for his part in the 1885 rebellion, a Canadian television show has questioned Poundmaker's conviction. The show, which aired in October 2002, used the original trial **transcripts** to re-create Poundmaker's trial on film. The filmmakers say that the historical records show that Poundmaker was innocent, and they have asked the Canadian justice department to review his case.

A Cree bush camp near Hudson Bay contains a mixture of traditional and modern objects. The lodge and stacked firewood contrast with the racy red snowmobile.

# James Bay Hydroelectric Project

In 1971, Quebec's premier, Robert Bourassa, began the James Bay Project **hydroelectric** dam, which flooded the rivers where the Crees still hunted and trapped. The Crees went to court to protest, and the judge agreed with the Crees. The rest of the project was stopped for twenty years.

In 1991, a different court allowed part of the project to continue, but it looked as if the whole project would never be completed due to the Cree protest. In 2002, however, the Grand Council of the Crees agreed to let Quebec finish the project, resulting in two huge dams to supply Quebec with electricity and provide jobs for the Crees. The project also pays the James Bay–area Cree bands large sums of money every year.

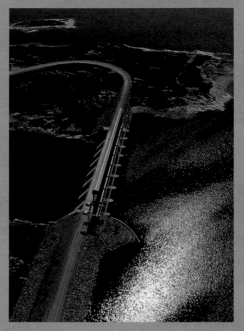

This photograph of the James Bay Hydroelectric Project, taken from the air, shows how huge the dam is and how large the area it affects.

However, even more traditional hunting, fishing, and trapping grounds have been flooded, most recently along a diversion of the Rupert River. In addition, mercury, a poisonous metal, dissolves into the water and is absorbed by the fish, which have sickened some of the Crees who have eaten them. Many Crees still feel that the project was not necessary and that alternative sources of energy, such as wind energy, could have been used. While the James Bay Hydroelectric Project is a blow to the Cree traditional lifestyle, the Cree bands are hoping that the payments and jobs will give them some new opportunities.

George Poitras, the chief of the Mikisew Cree Nation, addresses crowds on Parliament Hill, Ottawa, in September 2011. This was part of a series of events in Canada and Washington, D.C., protesting the development of oil mining in Alberta and the construction of oil pipelines across Canada and the United States.

## CRUDE OIL CRISIS

Bitumen, a thick and sticky type of crude oil, has been mined in Alberta since 1967. As fuel supplies decline elsewhere in the world, businesses are now looking to Alberta for their supplies. Unfortunately, this oil is full of poisonous chemicals, which have polluted rivers in the mining process. To make a barrel of refined oil uses a great deal of energy and produces large quantities of carbon dioxide gas, one of the main causes of climate change. The oil industry affects the lives of many Cree groups in Alberta.

## THE LUBICON CREE DISASTER

The pipelines that take the oil across the continent are also a danger because there are regular leaks. In April 2010, a spill of 28,000 barrels of crude oil leaked into the forests and bogs around Little Buffalo, Alberta, a Lubicon Cree community. The fumes caused feelings of sickness, headaches, and burning eyes among the Crees. The Lubicon Crees have never benefited from the oil wells on their land. Their water comes from the surrounding area and is now poisoned.

## HEALTH CONCERNS FOR THE MIKISEW CREES

The Mikisew Crees of Fort Chipewyan depend on the Athabasca River. It provides them with drinking water and fish, but it is highly polluted as a result of crude oil production. The Crees have noticed that many of the fish are now deformed. They have also realized that more people are getting ill than previously, some with a rare cancer. The Mikisew Crees believe the oil industry is to blame.

## MONTANA FLOODS

In June 2010, flooding on the Rocky Boy Indian Reservation in Montana caused considerable damage. Water mains broke, leaving the people without drinking water, and some homes were badly damaged. The health center was worst affected, and a temporary clinic had to be set up. Three weeks later, President Obama declared the reservation a disaster area. This allowed the Chippewa Cree Tribe to claim money to repair buildings, roads, and the water supplies.

## A MIX OF CULTURES

The Crees continue to fight to maintain their traditional culture and teach their children the Cree language and the importance of living off the land. The difficulty of balancing a life as a wage earner and the desire to go out into the bush to hunt and trap is an issue most Crees face today, since few can make their living as full-time hunters and trappers. As their prosperity and education increase, the Crees have more choices, and they are choosing to embrace their traditional culture and values whenever they can.

When you're in the bush, you're not just there to learn how to set a trap, how to hunt moose and caribou or how to set a net. It's about how you take care of yourself and how you deal with yourself in your life.

*Robert Jimiken, a senior Cree hunter and trapper, 1998*

During a visit from Great Britain's Prince Charles, Cree women dress in their finest traditional clothes to honor him.

# TIMELINE

| | |
|---|---|
| 1600 | Cree population totals between fifteen and thirty thousand. |
| 1670 | Hudson's Bay Company sets up trading posts in Cree territory. Crees begin to exchange furs for guns and horses. |
| 1670–1810 | Crees expand their territory to the southwest, and the Plains Cree buffalo-hunting lifestyle begins. |
| 1781 | Smallpox epidemic kills many Crees. |
| 1810–50 | Plains Cree Horse Wars against other tribes. |
| 1870s | Buffaloes are wiped out by American hunting. |
| 1870 | Canada purchases land from Hudson's Bay Company. |
| 1871 | Blackfeet defeat Plains Crees at the Battle of Old Man River. |
| 1876 | Poundmaker becomes chief of a Cree band. |
| 1876–1906 | Cree bands sign treaties with the Canadian government, giving up most of their lands in exchange for reserves and social services. |
| 1880s | Christian missionaries begin converting the Plains Crees to Christianity. |
| 1884–1921 | Sun Dance is outlawed in Canada. |
| 1885 | Louis Riel leads the Métis against the Canadian government; a Cree sympathizer, Poundmaker, is found guilty of treason. |
| 1916 | Rocky Boy Indian Reservation established in Montana for displaced Crees from Canada and Chippewas (Ojibwes) from North Dakota. |
| 1920–1940 | Crees are hit hard by measles and flu epidemics. |
| 1940s–70 | Cree children are sent to boarding schools to learn English. |

1958  John Tootoosis and others found Federation of Saskatchewan Indians.

1971  Quebec begins James Bay hydroelectric dam project; Crees protest.

1974  Grand Council of the Crees is formed to represent the Crees of James Bay and northern regions of Quebec.

1984  The Chippewa-Cree tribe of the United States creates the Stone Child Community College.

1990s  Canadian First Nations and Canadian government review original treaties and try to settle remaining issues.

1991  Crees protest plans to expand James Bay hydroelectric project.

1994  Quebec government cancels the hydroelectric project.

2002  Grand Council of the Crees agreement with Quebec government allows James Bay hydroelectric dam project to be finished in exchange for Cree employment in the industry and large sums of money for development of Cree communities. The agreement includes sharing of revenues and joint management of mining, forestry, and hydroelectric resources in Cree lands in Quebec.

2005  Chippewa Cree Rocky Boy Indian Reservation has 5,656 enrolled members.

2007  Chippewa Cree Tribe opens a casino near Box Elder, Montana.

2010  Population of Rocky Boy Indian Reservation reaches 3,323. The reservation is declared a disaster area after severe storms and flooding. The health center, roads, and water systems are damaged.

2011  Opening of the Aanischaaukamikw Cultural Institute (an architect-designed Cree museum) in Oujé-Bougoumou, Quebec.

# GLOSSARY

**activist:** someone who believes in direct action to support or oppose a controversial issue.

**allied:** agreeing to work together for a common goal.

**ancestors:** people from whom an individual or group is descended.

**boarding school:** a place where children must live at the school.

**breechcloths:** strips of cloth worn around the hips.

**convert:** to cause a person to change a belief, usually a religious one.

**culture:** arts, beliefs, and customs that make up a people's way of life.

**descendants:** all the children and children's children of an individual.

**dialects:** types of language that are spoken by particular groups or in particular areas.

**discrimination:** unjust treatment, usually because of a person's race or sex.

**environment:** objects and conditions all around that affect living things and communities.

**epidemic:** a sudden increase of a rapidly spreading disease.

**floodplain:** the area of land beside a river or stream that is covered with water during a flood.

**hide:** the skin of an animal.

**hydroelectric:** having to do with the use of flowing water to generate electricity.

**ice age:** a period of time when the earth is very cold and lots of water in the oceans turns to ice.

**irrigation:** any system for watering the land to grow plants.

**medicine man:** a spiritual or religious leader who has the power to heal.

**migration:** movement from one place to another.

**missions:** churches or other buildings where people of one religion try to teach their beliefs to people of another religion.

**nation:** people who have their own customs, laws, and land separate from other nations or peoples.

**pemmican:** a food made from dried meat pounded into powder and mixed with melted fat.

**persecution:** treating someone or a certain group of people badly over a period of time.

**powwow:** a celebration of Indian culture, usually including singing, drumming, dancing, giving thanks, and connecting with loved ones.

**prejudice:** dislike or injustice that is not based on reason or experience.

**puberty:** the time of physical changes in the human body when a girl becomes a woman or a boy becomes a man.

**reservation:** land set aside by the U.S. government for specific Native American tribes to live on.

**reserves:** land set aside by the Canadian government for First Nations (Native American) tribes.

**self-sufficient:** needing no outside help for basic things like food.

**sinew:** a piece of tough fibrous tissue in an animal's body that joins a muscle to a bone or a bone to another bone.

**smallpox:** a disease that causes a high fever and small bumps.

**social services:** services provided by the government or other organizations to help the poor or sick.

**spiritual:** affecting the human spirit or religion rather than physical things.

**supernatural:** beyond the natural world; something that cannot be seen, especially relating to gods and spirits.

**sweetgrass:** a hardy grass that smells like vanilla when dried.

**transcripts:** exact records, in writing, of an event.

**travois:** a long sled formed by two poles with a platform between them.

**treason:** the act of betraying one's country.

**treaties:** agreements among two or more nations.

**visions:** things seen or experienced that are not from this world but the supernatural one; they resemble dreams, but the person is awake.

# MORE RESOURCES

## WEBSITES:

**http://collections.civilisations.ca/public/pages/cmccpublic/alt-emupublic/Query.php?lang=0**
Search the Canadian Museum of Civilization for photos of hundreds of historic Cree artifacts.

**http://www.canadahouse.com/dynamic/artists/Allen_Sapp.asp**
Images of works by Cree artist Allen Sapp.

**http://www.canadahouse.com/dynamic/artists/Jane_Ash_Poitras.asp**
Images of works by Cree artist Jane Ash Poitras.

**http://www.bigorrin.org/cree_kids.htm**
Online Cree Indian Fact Sheet for Kids in question-and-answer form with useful links.

**http://www.creeculture.ca**
Follow the links to learn more about the Cree people and their language, arts, and traditional ways.

**http://www.creeculture.ca/content/resources/en/details.php?category[]=Hoods&browse**
Photos of traditional Cree clothing.

**http://www.creeculture.ca/content/resources/en/hphotos.php**
Find historical photos of the Crees.

**http://www.georgelittlechild.com/3.htm**
The website of artist George Littlechild.

**http://www.manataka.org/page103.html#Introduction%20to**
All about the games of the Plains Crees.

**http://www.mistissini.ca/welcome.html**
The website of the Cree Nation of Mistissini in Quebec has pages about the land and culture with many modern photos.

**http://www.nationnews.ca/**
The website of *Nation*, the online Cree newspaper.

**http://www.native-languages.org/cree.htm**
This website has links to online Cree language resources.

**http://www.native-languages.org/cree_animals.htm**
Photos of animals with their Cree names and a pronunciation guide.

**http://www.ncncree.com/ncn/histgallery/index.html**
Historic Nisichawayasihc Cree Nation photos.

**http://www.nemaska.com/**
The website of the Cree Nation of Nemaska in Quebec has a tribal history and many modern photos.

**http://www.ouje.ca/content/index.php**
Website of the Oujé-Bougoumou Cree Nation, with information about and photos of their architect-designed village.

**http://www.sicc.sk.ca/index.html**
The website of the Saskatchewan Indian Cultural Centre has lots of information on the different Cree groups.

## BOOKS:

Banting, Erin. *Cree (Aboriginal Peoples)*. Weigl Publishers Inc., 2010.

Bial, Raymond. *The Cree (Lifeways)*. Benchmark Books, 2006.

Bjorklund, Ruth. *The Cree (First Americans)*. Marshall Cavendish Children's Books, 2008.

Bouchard, David. *Qu'Appelle*. Raincoast Books, 2002.

Bouchard, David, and Allen Sapp. *The Song Within My Heart*. Raincoast Books, 2003.

Gibson, Karen Bush. *Native American History for Kids: With 21 Activities*. Chicago Review Press, 2010.

King, David C. *First People*. DK Children, 2008.

Murdoch, David S. *North American Indian (DK Eyewitness Books)*. DK Children, 2005.

Riehecky, Janet. *The Cree Tribe (Native Peoples)*. Capstone Press, 2002.

Ryan, Maria Felkins, and Linda Schmittroth. *Cree (Tribes of Native America)*. Blackbirch Press, 2003.

# THINGS TO THINK ABOUT AND DO

## CREE CLOTHING

Read about the different kinds of clothing worn by the Western Woods Crees and the Plains Crees. Draw a picture showing the differences in clothing between the Cree cultural groups. Why did they dress differently? Why do they wear the kinds of clothes that they do?

## HONORING A TREATY

In the 1870s, many Cree bands signed treaties with the government, giving up their traditional lands for assigned reservations and social services such as food, tools, schools, and doctors. What can the Crees do if the government doesn't keep its side of the bargain? Form a small discussion group and discuss what you think their choices are.

## ROLE PLAYING

Poundmaker was accused of treason, or disloyalty to the government, because of his part in Riel's rebellion. In a group, act out the trial with students taking the parts of the two lawyers, the judge, and Poundmaker. Other students can be the jury. What do you think each of these people was thinking and feeling during the trial?

## NAME YOURSELF

Plains Cree children often had two names: their "real" name and an everyday name that was descriptive of what they looked like, what they were good at, or something that happened to them. If you were a Plains Cree, what do you think your everyday name would be and why? Write a paragraph explaining your name.

# INDEX